the darkness of spring

*what lies beyond
the shadow*

the darkness of spring

*what lies beyond
the shadow*

by Jenna Bushspies

design & illustration by AnnaMarie Salai
West Finch, LLC

The Darkness of Spring: What Lies Beyond the Shadow
copyright © 2022 by Jenna Bushspies

Printed in the United States of America.
All rights reserved, including the right of reproduction in whole or in part, in any form, except in the case of reprints in the context of reviews.

Designed by AnnaMarie Salai of West Finch
www.westfinch.com

dedicated to the
goddess within you —
and me

contents

I —————— 21

II —————— 67

III —————— 91

IV —————— 123

V —————— 155

intro

When my skin and bone begin to crumble, I hope the one thing people remember about me is my story and the impact I had on others. Sometimes, this could be as little as a smile on one of their hardest days, or as big as the love we shared. My goal for this book is to use my voice to make at least one person feel not so alone during their time on this earth.

My parents separated at the age of five. The divorce was violent and chaotic. This was mostly due to my biological father having anger issues. After 26 trips around the sun, I came to terms with the fact that this was abuse. It took a long time to come to terms with the fact that one of the people I thought loved me unconditionally, was someone completely different in the light.

From when I was eleven until now, I have suffered from depression, bulimia, anorexia, anxiety; all of which were a result of my C-PTSD. Trauma from over the years, manifested as memories, self-loathing, and self harm.

My healing journey has led me to rediscover my voice and what it means to be authentically me.

Learning to reclaim my power has caused me to cross paths with Persephone over the years. When I was younger something about her story beckoned me. It wasn't until I older, that I realized why...

Persephone's story is that of autonomy and duality. She is the Goddess of the spring and Queen of the underworld. Her story goes, she is kidnapped after her father makes a deal with her uncle, Hades, who is in love with her. He kidnaps her to the underworld.

Her departure from the earth above results in fall and winter. Hades offers her a pomegranate, the fruit of the underworld, to which she obliges to eat— this trickery causing Persephone to stay in the underworld for half the year. The other half, she is to return to the surface.

Was Persephone kidnapped?

Or did she have a choice in her departure from earth?

Did she love Hades to begin with?

Did she fall in love with his darkness, and in turn, her own?

Did the underworld finally offer her a place where she could be out of the shadow of her mother, Demeter, and father, Zeus— a place where she could reign as an equal with a partner? To what extent was she forced into her roles as Persephone, Goddess of the spring, and Persephone, Queen of the underworld?

From my perspective, Persephone's story poses the question of accepting one's shadow and reclaiming one's power from within. The shadow part of the self is everything about oneself that one rejects, tries to repress, and, in turn, projects onto others.

The light part of the self is exactly the opposite; it is everything one accepts about themselves and shows to the world. In Persephone's story, she must come to terms with her power, her darkness, and her light. Her story spoke to me, because this is the work I needed to do in order to break out of the role I was raised to fit.

Persephone and I were both raised to be quiet, good girls, cast in their parents' shadows. Never to overpower or outshine them. Did Persephone or I have a choice in our stories?

Regardless of this answer, we learned how to speak our truth, shine our light, and make peace with our darkness.

I

fall of persephone:

consumed by the darkness

thoughts of a depressed shell of a human

Depression is...hard to explain to those who never have felt its gentle but cold embrace. After awhile, it becomes comforting, like the socks you continue to wear even though your feet get sores where the holes expose your skin. It's like smoking cigarettes, using drugs; its darkness can be addicting. It might make me sound crazy, but this world might make you go mad.

The following is a journal entry from one of my deepest black holes — when I refused therapy, meds, isolated myself from friends and family, swallowed by my bad habits of drugs, eating disorders, and drinking...

...just to numb the pain for a few hours.

these fucking stupid metaphors

"you will pull yourself out one reach at a time"

"you are stronger than you know"

it's fucking stupid

it drives me mad

the hope

the stupidity

the ignorance

"wish i could say i wasn't feeling how you're feeling, i'm so off this week"

"i'm not exactly getting through life unscathed either"

"awh i'm so sorry"

these people

these simple-minded fuckers

"what triggered it?"

the humidity

i worked out

i went to work

then

s
   l
      o
         w
            l
               y

                   faded

i had a cup of chips and pineapple

at 5 am

it's 7 pm

everything is heavy

so heavy

poured a glass of wine to numb myself

but it's heavy too

looking at the glass

imagining the warmth spreading

through my whole body

entering my throat

the potent bitter red consuming me

but

what's the point

it will numb me

for all of 30 seconds

then it sets back in

the lump in my throat

the tears well up

i push them down

staring

for hours

at the walls

at the ceiling

at the floor

the rug

the next day

i'm a fuse

that can't be put out

to be productive at the most unproductive, useless things

cleaning and sorting receipts at midnight

sorting through all my electronics at one a.m. because

my new mouse doesn't have batteries

and i can't sleep

knowing that

i try to sleep

but

something

keeps me up

i NEED

a new painting

the urge overpowers me

i search 12 websites

which one?

this one?

that one?

the fifth one?

the purple one?

does this have too many flowers?

too feminine?

too masculine?

too many colors?

too interpretive?

end up

not

buying

a

damn

thing

i'm supposed to go out tomorrow

but

i don't want to

to have conversations

that lead to nothing

this notebook

is the only one

listening

and it doesn't have to say a thing

maybe i don't need reassurance

explanations

i maybe just need

someone to sit quietly with me

slow breathing

my chest

rises

and

falls

the wifi blinks

it's calming

unlike humans

and sounds

nothing is calming

i am nothing

i am withdrawing

from society

social interactions

but i do what they tell me

exercise

eat healthy

stop drinking (as much)

stop smoking (as much)

but

i still

can't

feel

anything

i am a

black hole

i am

suffocating

in a box full of air

how can this be

maybe one day

there's really just no point

we live

and then

we die

we are robotic

programmed

tanned

and dyed

glaring white teeth

UV ray kissed skin

words are exchanged

questions are asked

the answers

—

ignored

what is the absence of emotion?

apathy

i am

..
    losing

        feeling

           ..

towards this life

and this life towards me

i no longer feel this or that

when they say *you're better*

you're different

they are deluding themselves

don't let them delude you

this is a game

you are the pawn

maybe one day

~~i'll be skinnier~~

~~i'll be prettier~~

~~i'll be smarter~~

~~i'll learn to love myself~~

i'll find someone who will read these words

and not fear the brutal and grotesque corners of my mind

and of reality

i'm not a pessimist

i'm not an optimist

i'm a realist

the first sign of pain

at the scene of the crime

wine on the table

cardboard in the trash

relishing in the last moments with you

maybe i can finally call myself an addict

addicted to even the toxicity of a relationship that was doomed before it began

it was never in our cards

we were never meant to be

it's hard to let go of something that felt like home

but you knew you never really had

i packed you away

pictures in a box

memories like a slideshow before unplugging the computer to clear the hard drive

reliving those last painful moments

over

and over

because

it's all i have left

of you

shattered

so many thoughts

memories

revelations

realizations

emotions, strong as the ocean to follow

anger

angry at you

for leaving

he asked me how you were

and the realization of losing the love we shared set in

mourning

minutes feel like hours

days feel like weeks

replaying our relationship

over and over

until i am consumed

tormented

today i longed for you

~~if you came back begging i would~~

but you won't

that's not how this works

my friends

my family

their love for me

is stronger than yours

maybe we weren't as happy as my mind likes

to make me believe

we used to want it to work

defy the odds against us

and make all the jokers lose their bets against us

but in the end

we lost the love we built

maybe we didn't build it strong enough

maybe we were always meant to fail

a box with a fragile warning

handle with care

dropped

and shattered

crying on the bathroom windowsill

Alone in a crowded room

An isolating feeling

With you I never felt that way

I felt your presence

I felt you

The quick glances

Looking at someone and knowing exactly what they are thinking

Now there's no one to look at

No one to hear my silent sentences

No one to hear my eyes screaming

I can't yell loud enough for them to hear

But you did

You heard my silence

Maybe I miss those feelings

Maybe I miss you

Maybe I miss the idea of you

I want to reach out

To hear you

But space and time heal they say

Is that bullshit

What we've always been told

Is it lies or scientific facts

Who knows

It's   all

bullshit   anyways

driving in an uber

Two weeks

Five days

Twenty two hours

I keep thinking you'll show up

On my doorstep

In my inbox

Telling me you made a mistake

You miss me

You love me

You want me and that's it

We'll figure it out

Together

Every time I get home

I let myself down

You aren't there

And you won't be

I need to let go of you

And who I've made you in my head

The you that is real

The you in my mind

Are different people

And I need to let them go

Because neither of them will ever show up

You aren't coming back

You aren't coming back

You aren't coming back

If I say it enough times maybe it will register in my brain

And I'll accept

That what we once were

Is packed away in a box in my bathroom

For good

the beginning

Tears spilling

Onto the floor

The calm after the storm

Purging of emotions

Anger

Fury

Rage

Love and loss

Loving him

Hating him

For making me care for someone

the way I always wished he cared for me

feb 27 2020

I'm not your fucking therapist

The words still singed in my mind

The cut still fresh

Every time I check my phone and you still haven't called

The knife goes a bit deeper

DO you care that I'm hurting

That've I've been hurt

That you hurt me

DO you care about the things that make me, me?

My empty home screen tells me you don't

But my heart says you do

To be young and naïve is a curse

Maybe I'm the crazy one

The toxic one

Maybe I have been wrong all along

Tell me you're sorry

Don't make me ask

Tell me not to worry

You were wrong

You made a mistake

You ~~couldn't~~ can't accept the parts of yourself you grew to hate

But maybe

You just can't accept these parts of me

I long for someone to ask

To listen

To understand

These wounds

These demons in my mind

That chase me down every night

Until they feast on my bones

I long for someone to be there

Like he was not

Like they were not

Like you ~~were~~ are not

Will you ever be

They all chose to turn a blind eye

You have too

Now that you saw a glimpse

Of what truly lies beneath my bones

My flesh

Layers of complexity

Not made for the light-hearted

But made for those who care

Truly, deeply care

About others

Not just you

Or me

But all the ones who suffer

angels & demons

it feels like you're listening
but you're not hearing me

the words spilling over my lips

pouring into the abyss before you

floating words

you; absorbed by your thoughts

our own stressors are always greater

larger

more difficult

more trifling

grander than the others'

when did struggle become a battle to the top?

as a child I thought we all had the inherent desire to help

embedded in our DNA

"if you pray hard enough,

the angels will answer your prayers"

to find a lost key

to put back together the pieces of my broken family

"pray when you wake up

and before you go to bed"

and help would supposedly show its face
when the time was right

what about the times crying in your bedroom at midnight

the moon shining on your tear covered cheeks

the time when your heart shattered for the millionth time

the moment when you realized

the demons are closer than you think

II

a goddess discovering her power:

finding myself in the darkness

out of touch

why is it such a big disappointment

when the people we love

cannot be who we have made them in our minds

how do we cope

with losing something that doesn't exist

do these fictional characters cause us to mix up reality

and imagination

maybe all along

i've fallen in love

with my dreams

and in turn

out of touch with reality

making peace with the shadow

it's wanting to hug your broken bones

and all that lies between them

it's making peace with the shadow that lurks in the night

it's walking with the angels

and the demons

it's beaming light and casting darkness

when Hyde comes out

seeking revenge on his enemies

it's learning the monsters they said lurked under the bed

are within us

and roam in broad daylight

not a damsel

I'm sad

I'm fucking mad

For not receiving the love I give

He trained me to suppress my needs

And to anticipate everyone else's

He trained me to think it's normal
to break your back in a relationship

Leaving it lopsided

it isn't fair

To love someone

To miss them

And to hate them

Maybe that's how the gods have cursed us

By making love a doubled-edged sword

Held the right way

It protects you, empowers you

A force that can be undefeatable

Held the opposing way

It can end your life

or keep you alive, just long enough to suffer for an eternity

They lied

They all fucking ~~lied~~ lie

There is no happy ending

True love was made to sell theater seats and sweatshirts

Be skinnier

Be blonder

Perfectly waxed and trimmed

You

The damsel

Will be saved by your prince

But I'm not a fucking damsel

Just a damaged shell of a creature

Pacing the Earth

To find what it means to be loved

I don't need to be saved

Just shown

That all the suffering wasn't for nothing

why do women

why do we women

think

we can

fix broken men

what is it about being a woman

that makes us feel

responsible

for their suffering

is it that

men

aren't supposed to cry

or is it that

we feel the need

to overcompensate

for how small

we actually feel

thoughts

what bothers me the most?

people who are needy, dependent, clingy,

people who constantly talk about themselves

why?

as a child i was never allowed to depend on my father

i was left to fend for myself

to be *independent*

when i would talk about myself, he would never care

i was never good enough

always could have done *better*

the A+ wasn't good enough

could have had an A++

i was never pretty **enough**

or smart **enough**

or fast **enough**

to be celebrated by him

so when people talk about themselves

i get mad

because why should they be celebrated if i never was

but

why can i not celebrate myself now?

what if i do?

will people find me conceited and selfish?

or will they see, the little me

finally honoring herself

maybe it isn't too late

maybe i'm not too far gone

what if this is just the beginning

of me

change

An era of change

For the world

For me

All the things they told me

are wrong

Why do I listen to them

I'm coming to realize

maybe

They are wrong

Maybe the only real person who sees the world as we do

Is ourselves

So why are we taught to live by
the clichés and standards
created by society

We are the keepers of our own truth

Holding the key to unlock our chains

Maybe after we realize that

we can look back and laugh

at all they made us believe

how will it end

directed

but unsure

wavering

questioning

how it will end

what should i do

will my next move be the right one

but right

is subjective

"it is always the right time to do the right thing"

maybe that is my sign

or maybe

it's just what they want me to believe in

false gods

and even falser hopes

pierce my skull

how will it end

we won't know

until it's too late

mirror

everything you are

is me

and everything i am

is you

you are simply a mirror of

my

                                              self

and

my shadow

III

persephone: queen of the underworld

when the darkness reclaimed me

the darkness that follows

They tell you, you don't need these pills

They think they know

But they don't know

What it's like

To push and push

And fall down

To do it all

And still fail

Because it always finds you

In the darkest corners of your mind

It taunts you on your brightest days

When you finally get what you want

It finds you

It reminds you

Nothing —

Nothing can fill this void

A gaping hole that can't be fixed

With surgery

or drugs

or love

or money

The ache so deep

It makes your guts wrench

A pain gifted to you with no remedy

It reminds you

How unworthy you are

Of all the things you want

How you will always be broken

And unfixable

It will always remind you

When you least expect it

A storm lasting not a day

Not a month

Not a week

But a lifetime

Yet only felt when it wants to be seen

When your demons feel neglected

They come out to play

To remind you

How comforting the darkness can be

reunited with the darkness

does it frighten you

to descry part of yourself

as if to meet again for the first time

only to rediscover

the corners of your mind

you swore you'd never return to

does it frighten you

when all too often

you find yourself

in the unspeakable

yet unforgettable

darkness

the comfort in loneliness

and its funny

how loneliness

can be consoling

and comfort can be found in despair

despair is the darkness's companion

it will lead you back home

to the edges of your mind

that are frightening

yet welcoming

because this is the only place

you can truly be yourself

a frank letter to the universe

what

is

this

what has become my life

a single mother of two

back in the place i tried so hard to run from

leaving him behind

somewhere in the haze of the last 365 days

i want to help

i started to identify as a therapist, a healer

now i'm just a suit and tie jane doe

to be lost in the current rushing in

any inkling of my existence

to be washed away at the high tide

with each wave slowly erasing

what i was working so hard for

it's gone

vanished

like a dream i cannot jump back into

something i can feel but cannot see

they say life only throws at you what you can handle

but i don't believe that's true

i can't look at a stranger's smile without tearing up

breaking down

you don't really know what someone is going through

by the look on their face

or their finely pressed button up shirt

look at me

look at him

look at her

my green little monster lights up

whenever i see that carefree smile

a feeling i so long for

to go to sunday brunch without a care

to leave home and not wonder how much time has passed

to go for a run and have the ability to do the extra mile

because the entire household is inside your body

i don't want them to go

i don't want them to stay

i miss the simplicity i took for granted

should have removed him from my life before this mess

i can't help but keep thinking

this **is**

my fault

if i would have left earlier

if i would have

done anything

different

would this be different

why must i always give up things for him

m
    o
        v
            i
                n
                    g

forward

and pivoting.

how does she do it

i hate when people ask

how does she do it

because i don't

i am a book, ripping at the seams

flooded

and

drained

at the same time

exploding

and

caving in

unable to cope

forced to adapt

losing feeling

going numb

devoid of emotion

wanting nothing

but

a chance to run

so fucking far

and never come back

the place

This Place

I've been here before

This place

Just me

I can't feel

I can't breathe

Knives in my chest

I choke on my words

My heart's in my throat

It feels like shattered glass cutting
with every thought of you

Look what you've done

Look what you've done

These scars

From each and every one of you

Like patchwork scattered
and piecemeal

I'm not supposed to feel this way

I'm not supposed to feel —

But I do

And I do

I try to get you off my mind

So I sleep in hopes my dreams will bring me to you again

I wake up

Drenched in sweat

Racing thoughts

Violent and hollow

Like the hole you left in me

You took my heart and you crumbled it in your hands

You crushed it

Squeezed it until it bled and broke

Maybe you broke me too

And now I'm left to clean up your mess

I've been here before

This place

The crime scene

Hues of yellows and reds

Sharp edges

Side glances

Avoid eye contact so you don't feel the pain you've caused

Dance around the words you planned to say

so you don't break my heart

It wasn't your fault

You weren't selfish

You weren't thinking

You didn't plan

For this

A tragic accident

Neither did I

Here I am in the eye of the storm

My fury and grief swirling around me

A hurricane of emotion and turmoil

So perfectly dancing around me

They say if you were raised in chaos

You will seek it out

I'm self-destructive

I tried to bury the urge

I tried to bury these feelings

I tried to keep my heart safe

But the storm door won't stay closed

And I am left to face the winds and rain

Alone

cat and mouse

how could you

reel me in

just to spit me out

did you enjoy

devouring me

piece by piece

my desires and terrors

my hopes and fears

was it a game

of cat and mouse

was it easy

are you satisfied

where is the trophy

the standing ovation

for your last act

the last hello

turned into the last goodbye

brush of the shoulder

to make up for the heartbreak

it wasn't any consolation

it wasn't an accident

you knew what you were doing

you did it so well

and as the curtain dropped

your swift and charming number

an exit so graceful

i almost forgot

how you spooned my heart out

with your bare hands

the maybes

how do you grieve losing something you never had

fuck the what ifs

the should haves

the maybes

fuck your sincerely messed up apology

that turned my idea of you to ashes

and burned my idea of you to the ground

the perfect game

you were my perfect game of ping pong

back   and   forth

across the table

a rehearsed exchange

but you pocketed the ball

and ended the game

confused

and dazed by your gracefully swift exit

he wasn't a god

he wasn't a god

he didn't sweep you off your feet

but he hastily left on his

you weren't in love

you loved the man you made him in your head

none of it was real

he was lonely

you were convenient

he wasn't who you thought

you didn't connect

                                        and you

                                                  were wrong

what describes a heart so broken

what words describe

a heart so broken

the pieces no longer fit together

what if the pieces never fit

what if this hole was always empty

and what i thought was broken

never even existed at all

sept. 18 2020

what are we

what is left of us

when all our suffering has gone

IV

persephone: hades' lover

realizing my darkness is just as important as my light

let's burn together

our hands clasped

our eyes locked

seconds turn to minutes turn to hours

words that go as deep as the hickory roots

that reach the fiery hell below us

let's burn together

how does it make you feel

how does it make you feel

when i open my mouth

and instead of your desires

my opinions come spilling out

how does it make you feel

when my, "No," bounces off the walls

does it scare you when i speak my truth

do my dreams and nightmares frighten you

does my autonomy threaten your fragile ego

i refuse to be your toy

your pawn

i am more than your play thing

i am a woman

i am a god

i am power

i am ablaze with the flames of a million hysterics

for so long

i fell into the role of the *good girl*

the nice girl

the sweet girl

to placate and to please was the mold i was raised to fit

how does it make you feel

when i

step out of your shadow

and into the light

for all the love

For all the Love I have

All the love I've had

All the love I've lost

All the love I've given

All the love I've received

All the love I've searched for

All the silent battles

All the tears

All the pain

All the happiness

Emotions as deep as the ocean

They are not my weakness

But my biggest strength

No matter how many times I'm struck down

No matter how many daggers pierce my heart

It will continue to beat

And its sound will echo

After everyone has gone

And there's nothing left

But me

when will i be enough

when will i be good enough

pretty enough

smart enough

nice enough

when will i be enough for a man

enough to receive the love i give

it feels wrong to crave love this gravely

when will i be enough for a man

to stay

rejection

triggers the wound deep inside me

the one he left me with

they say there is no greater a love,

than a father's for his children

they didn't know about the love he had for himself

"you're a jerk"

"you've gained weight"

"you could have done better"

his words

his voice

consume my mind

when someone else reminds me

i am not enough

every day i draw my sword on the battle field

slashing through each intrusive thought

each day i defend my mind

just to stay alive

i hope all the love you robbed me of

gets pulled out from under you

i hope your perfect facade you hide behind

gets destroyed

and in return for all the suffering you caused

the universe pays me in gold

i refuse to beg at the foot of a man

who doesn't realize my worth

i have come to realize my worth is not dependent

on anyone's approval

but my own

is it wrong

is it wrong

to crave a connection so vast and deep

like a cavern that only we can find

in the depths of our souls

voltaic

like a lightning bolt that turns sand to glass

something only we would bear witness to

a secret bond that no one can touch

is it wrong

to want desire
to overpower
the little free will i have left

is it wrong

to want someone to consume me so deeply

they learn me better than i can ever learn myself

i've been told

maybe i have yet to learn

how love can turn into chaos

and passion and desire into devious intent

i've read

when you feel this way

you need to find yourself

maybe you are the one you are searching for

~~at the bottom of the bottle~~

and when you find yourself

it will all seemingly make sense

every heartbreak

every ending

all the lies and what you thought was love

all of it will seemingly make sense

to find what was buried underneath

not my fault

it's not my fault

none of this is my fault

here's a toast

to all of the guilt you gave me

to every broken glass

to every slur you called me

to the hitting, choking, lunging

to the punishment, so brutal and cold

to the death threats

to every damn thing you've ever done

it's not my fault

none of it is

it's your fault

and one day when you realize

it will be too late

for i've already slipped out of your grasp

and into my power

if we only knew

If only we could know

the last time we saw someone

Would we hug them a little longer

Listen to their laugh a little closer

Put all your favorite memories on a reel in your mind

Press your cheek next to theirs a few seconds longer

Kiss them a little harder

Memorize the lines on their face as they smile

Maybe if we knew

Would we still take them for granted

Maybe if we knew

We would make sure to love them a little better

realizations

I realized

I place my worth on others' opinions

The opinions of men, who ask for a glimpse,

before they buy the ticket

I seek approval and validation

for my entire existence

on men

But

Why

Look at the life I, a woman, built

I think I'm ugly

I place the weight of my worth on my physical appearance

Maybe, just maybe, I am starting to finally see my beauty

But maybe not

Beauty is a construct built by society

Fleeting and subjective

I am learning to love my fragmented pieces

In between the fragmented frames of life

I couldn't have changed him

Even if I loved him more

I couldn't have changed

any of them

I loved them more than they deserved

revelations

Revelations

I place my worth on your opinion

On his opinion

I seek approval and validation

for my entire existence

from him

Why?

Look at the life I built without them

The beauty I failed to acknowledge for so long

Is budding like a flower as I heal

What is beauty?

Is it simply a construct

Or does it exist

I am learning to love myself

Unconditionally

It feels —

comfortable

I couldn't have changed him

I couldn't have changed any of them

I am let down when people don't fit the molds I create for them in my mind

I fictionalize people and their lives

A grand performance in my head

Deserves a standing ovation

From no one

But me

monday night revelations

why am i so obsessed with love

who is that

me?

the little girl who never was enough

for him

rose colored glasses

why do i make people feel like home

before i know them

their demons they talk to late at night

maybe i never loved anyone at all

maybe i only ever loved the idea of loving

and being loved

and every man i've ever met has been tinted with rose

our potential

what is it we fear about our potential

is it the power

maybe it's scarier to think about what we could be

than all that we are

because all that we are is real

and all that we could be is gold

a field of daisies

you pretended our love was a treasure only we could find

turns out you can't turn a field of daises into gold

the light of the moon will never compare to that of the sun

you have me done

with men feasting on my heart

like a piece of primed meat

the allure of the hunt

like that of a shiny precious jewel

but if you get too close

the shards of my broken heart

reflect your true intentions

back at you

when the devil comes knocking

when the devil comes knocking

take heed

he'll steal your heart

faster than you can sell your soul

you'll be eating out of his palm

it only took two days

for me to love all of his darkness

his shadow and all

he kissed my forehead

caressed my cheek

and whispered in my ear

"be my queen"

he made me feel

as if i were

everything i ever wanted to believe i was

i know the one before was safe and "good"

but you are mistreated and misunderstood

you are everything i crave to love

"be mine"

said the devil

and i obliged

our love hath no weakness

for it is forged by darkness and fire

the type of love that cannot be tamed by a man

"til the flames turn our flesh to ash"

he said

and into his fiery kingdom we rode

V

persephone: queen of spring
and queen of the underworld

falling in love with my darkness

the end of his reign

The end of his Reign

Why did you create this mess

Why am I stepping on shards of broken glass

I thought I was out from under your grip

Here I am in this prison all the same

How can you love someone who hurt(s) you

Over and Over

Like an infant banging their head on the crib

Sometimes self-soothing

A double-edged sword

Resembling agony to onlookers

A shard of glass embedded in my flesh

Holding back the sea of blood that inhabits my body

If I removed it

Would the blood pour out

And leave me hollow

Would it take away the memories of you with it

Would it take your voice, soft and patient

Would it take your hands

That caught me when I fell

Would it take your words

Darling, princess, daughter

Would it take your empty promises

Would it take your insincere apologies

Would it wash away the guilt

That eats me alive in my sleep

Would it wash away the grief

Of losing you forever

Your memory haunting me

The knight in shining armor

turned out to be the captor

I'm not a princess

You were never a king

This marks the end of your Reign over me

to forgive and not forget

to forgive and forget

is what they told me

but i didn't listen

i wrote about your crimes

i screamed on rooftops

i shattered your vases and plates and bottles

i burned every picture of you i owned

i cut you out of my heart

but not out of my head

the affliction you caused will live on in my mind

the emotions so clear and crisp

they cut through my haziest thoughts

every memory is like a jagged edge

piercing each bubble of hope i had of you

pinned down by the daggers you used to cut me

your ugly words

the names

the insults

the threats

don't worry

i'll forgive

but not forget

signs of healing

wanting love

wanting to be worth it

it's hard to believe i am enough

when i was never enough

for

him

i know he was wrong

but how do i prove to myself i am whole

maybe this was his grand plan

to trick me into thinking

i always needed someone else

like

him

i was always taught

my self worth depended on how i served

him

did he want me

to be his daughter

did he want to

be my father

or did he want

a servant

someone whose role was to placate him

at the slight of distress

my own needs cast in my shadow

but now

i am woman

hear me fucking roar

my own needs and desires

springing from the top of my lungs

like flowers overflowing, outgrowing

their original pot

filled to the brim with love

maybe everything i need

has

                always

                                      been

within me

maybe i have been taught to weigh the external

more than it actually weighed

maybe i can learn

to live in my honor and worth

maybe i have always been enough

maybe he made me feel empty

because to him

i was only there to make him feel full

maybe i have found my power

and it is time to reclaim my throne

a letter to my mother

red sky at night

sailor's delight

you would say

reassuring me the sky wouldn't make any noises tonight

and tomorrow

the sun would reappear

there would be no storms

but the storms came anyway

despite your promise

it wasn't your fault

some things are out of our control

like the holes in the ceiling

gaping wide open

like the broken doors

torn apart at the hinge

like the shattered glass

whose sound echoed in the staircase

they all became the scars

we said we couldn't see

i'm sorry falls off your lips into my lap

an apology for the things

and the people

that we could not control

you fail to remember

the things you did control

like the way you held me in the basement

and the strength you had

because sometimes the darkest moments

remind us the stars aren't too far off

and maybe

if they hug us tight enough

we forget the storm

and fall back soundly asleep

the one

i used to believe *the one* existed

i thought it was him

i thought it was you

i mistook the devil for an angel

and called him mine

but she stole your heart

and took you away

the last to role call

late to the show

her act exquisite

fit the role so perfectly

she looked like flowers

sauntering gracefully across the stage

her eyes like fire

her voice intoxicating

i looked in the mirror

and she

was me

i didn't know all along

that i was the one

who could love me

for me

how could i not know

what i longed for all this time

was not the love of another

but the love i had within

they don't advertise it

they can't sell something you can't see

so they sell diamonds

and roses

and cars

and mansions

the one thing you need

and crave the most

money can't buy

you can't make it in a factory

but you can make it with

pages and canvases

colors and words

heartache and love

anguish

fear

love

mixed with blood sweat and tears

this is what it takes

for you

to crawl back

to yourself

back

to your home

the bottom of the bathtub

drops of water on my palms

soaking the pages in front of me

beads of cabernet on my lips

leaving behind stains of crimson red

rediscovering my roots at the bottom of the bathtub

stretching deep below the surface

flowers billowing

branches

leaves

and vines

s   p   r   e   a   d   i   n   g

e
  x
    p
      a
        n
          d
            i
              n
                g

until I find Her in the silence

this body is home

this body is more than my flesh and bones

it is more than the sum of my scars

and crooked nose

it is a soldier

recovering from battle

it is a lover of a thousands hearts

it is a home

to my fears and hopes and desires

it is more than the bumps and bruises that lay on my skin

it is a home

for a soul made of hues of the rainbow

fluorescent as daylight

stronger than every precious metal combined

it is a vessel to my no longer fragile heart

its walls held together by a spirit

that's conquered dragons and demons in her darkest nights

it is a home

that's withstood a thousand and one storms

never fallen victim to the vicious winds of the outside world

it is a home

for me

a reminder to not barter your worth

sometimes

you just need a gentle reminder

not to barter your worth

you are not a precious metal

you are a heart

and lungs

and skin

and bone

you are love

you are more than the sum of your parts

you are worth more than a thousand sunsets

don't let them make you forget

you are worth it

to me

i deserve

I deserve to be loved

Not liked

Not lusted after

Not settled for

But Loved

worth in a broken heart

I've finally found my worth in a broken heart

How tragically ironic

My truth

My power

All came spilling out

When you left

My world of dormant potentials

This is not our time

This is my time

I've had the universe show me time and time again

Not to let the direction of my life

rest on the indecisions of a man

I have finally learned my lesson

I'm not afraid anymore

To be without the love of a man

Whether it be of you

Or of my father

I was born with all the love I need inside of me

And I thank you

For helping me see

Just exactly who I want to be

thank you

This book is a reflection of me and my heart.

Thank you Anna for helping make this dream come to life. Thank you for all the late nights and incredible collaboration.

Thank you to everyone I've crossed paths with; you have inspired me to see beyond my eyes.

Thank you to my mother for protecting and loving me despite my flaws.

Thank you to my siblings, Anastasia, Rjay, and John, for teaching me what it means to love without bounds.

Thank you to you—the reader—for supporting my journey.

about the writer

Jenna Bushspies was born on June 26, 1995 and resides in Pennsylvania, USA. She has been writing poetry and short stories since she was 8 years old as an outlet for her overflowing emotions. Never in a million years did she see herself as a writer, as an artist. She thought of herself as someone who used writing to cope with life's messy uncertainties and chaos.

Jenna decided to release her story after unexpectedly becoming a foster mother to her three siblings during the COVID-19 pandemic. At the age of 26, this event turned her world upside down. Jenna started to share her story and realized people were actually interested in hearing what she had to share. Ultimately, this led to the production and release of this, Jenna's first book.

After attending Drexel University in Philadelphia, PA for a B.S. in Mathematics, Jenna now has her own tutoring business that specializes in math tutoring for all ages. In her free time, she likes to tutor, write, stay physically active, cuddle with her dog, Huxley, and spend time with family and friends.

jennabushspies.com

follow me on Instagram
@jennabushspies

www.ingramcontent.com/pod-product-compliance
Lightning Source LLC
Chambersburg PA
CBHW022012290426
44109CB00015B/1152